IGUANAS

by Kathryn Stevens

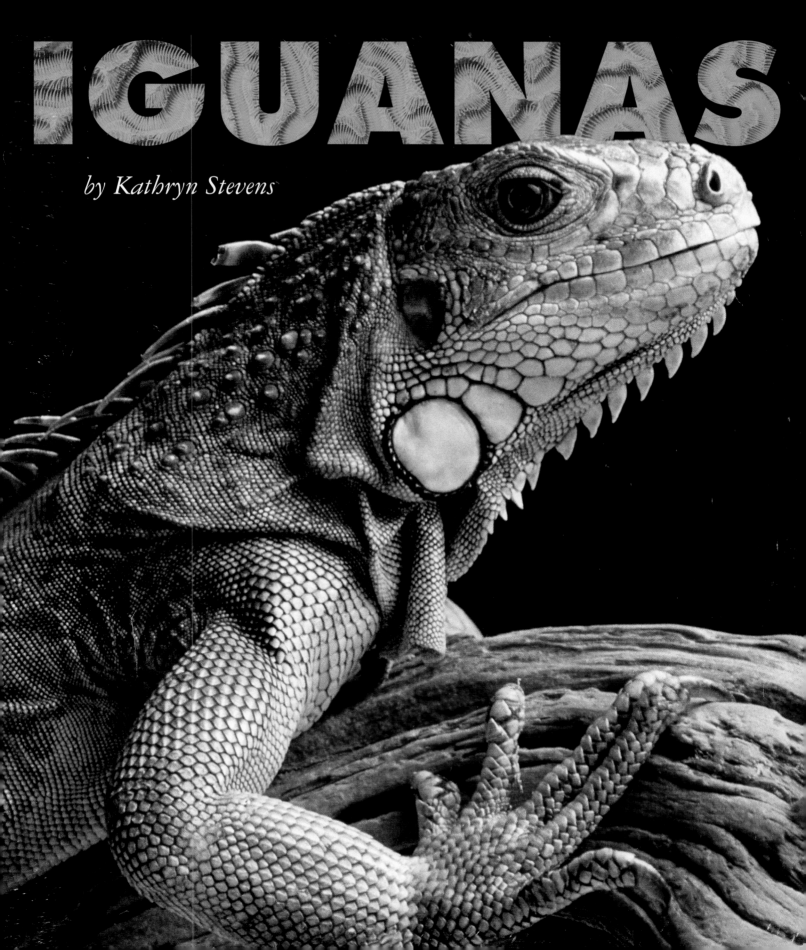

Published in the United States of America by The Child's World®
1980 Lookout Drive • Mankato, MN 56003-1705
800-599-READ • www.childsworld.com

PHOTO CREDITS
© Brandon Cole Marine Photography/Alamy: 10
© DANI/JESKE/Animals Animals–Earth Scenes: 16–17
© Dave and Sigrun Tollerton/Alamy: 18–19
© Henry Beeker/Alamy: 27
© James Schwabel/Alamy: 20
© John Crum/Alamy: 7
© Kennan Ward/Corbis: 15
© Kevin Schafer/Alamy: 11
© Kim Taylor/naturepl.com: 24
© Luiz Claudio Marigo/naturepl.com: 4–5
© M. Timothy O'Keefe/Alamy: 12, 13
© Mike Powell/Getty Images: 23
© Tim Fitzharris/Minden Pictures: 28
© Watts/Hall, Inc./Corbis: cover, 1
© Zigmund Leszczynski/Animals Animals–Earth Scenes: 9

ACKNOWLEDGMENTS
The Child's World®: Mary Berendes, Publishing Director;
Katherine Stevenson, Editor; Pamela Mitsakos, Photo Researcher;
Judy Karren, Fact Checker

The Design Lab: Kathleen Petelinsek, Design; Kari Tobin, Page Production

LIBRARY OF CONGRESS CATALOGING-IN-PUBLICATION DATA
Stevens, Kathryn, 1954–
  Iguanas / by Kathryn Stevens.
      p. cm. — (New naturebooks)
  Includes index.
  ISBN 978-1-59296-848-0 (library bound : alk. paper)
  1. Iguanas—Juvenile literature. I. Title.
  QL666.L25S74 2007
  597.95'42—dc22   2007015320

Table of Contents

On the cover: This green iguana is resting on a piece of driftwood.

Meet the Iguana!

To protect themselves, green iguanas sometimes snap their jaws or whip their tails. To escape an enemy, they can even lose part of their tail, and it will grow back!

Green iguanas swim well. They like branches that hang over water. If an enemy comes, they dive into the water to get away.

Sunlight filters down through the moist, green leaves of a Central American rain forest. High above the ground, the treetops form a thick cover. A big greenish **lizard** is crawling along one of the branches. It has a long tail and a row of spines down the middle of its back. With its coloring, the lizard is hard to see against the leaves and branches. The lizard nibbles on a leaf, then heads for a tasty piece of fruit. What is this treetop lizard? It's an iguana!

This green iguana is climbing on a branch in Venezuela.

4

What Are Iguanas?

Half or more of an iguana's length is in its tail.

Some iguanas can grow to 6 feet (2 m) long.

Many iguanas are good at climbing trees. Their long, sharp claws give them a good grip.

"Iguana" is a common name for a number of different types of lizards. Like all modern lizards, iguanas are cold-blooded, egg-laying **reptiles** with four legs and a long tail. Their skin is dry and covered with hard **scales**. Iguanas tend to have spines on their backs and flaps of loose skin called *dewlaps* on their throats. Their eardrums are on the outsides of their heads. Their feet have five toes with sharp claws.

Iguanas are found mostly in North, Central, and South America. Some also live on islands in the Caribbean Sea and the Pacific Ocean, and on Madagascar off the coast of Africa. They live in lots of different **habitats**, from deserts to seacoasts to warm, wet forests.

This iguana lives on the island of Bonaire. You can clearly see the dewlap hanging from its throat.

Are There Different Kinds of Iguanas?

The "rock iguana" group includes blue iguanas, Cuban iguanas, rhinoceros iguanas, Jamaican iguanas, and several others.

When a green iguana feels threatened, it sticks out its dewlap to make itself look bigger and scarier.

A green iguana can fall out of a 40-foot (12 m) tree without getting hurt.

There are many different kinds, or **species**, of iguanas. Scientists group related species together. For example, *Cyclura* is a group of closely related "rock iguanas" from the West Indies. Ideas on how iguanas should be grouped keep changing. The general iguana family has some 650 species. They vary a lot in their size, what they look like, and how they live.

Green iguanas are the kind people know best. These lizards grow to 6 or even 7 feet (about 2 m) in length. They're common in warm, moist forests throughout Central and South America. Although they can swim well and move quickly on land, they spend most of their time high in the trees. Their color ranges from dull to bright green.

You can see the scaly skin and spines on this green iguana.

You can see how different this chuckwalla looks compared to the iguanas on pages 9 and 10.

Some iguanas live in dry regions instead. Spiny-tailed iguanas, or ctenosaurs, live in dry, open places in Central America. They grow up to 36 inches (91 cm) long. Unlike most iguanas, they live in groups. Desert iguanas and chuckwallas live in the Mojave and Sonoran Deserts of the U.S. and Mexico. They do well in hot sun that would send most lizards running for the shade!

The Galápagos Islands off the South American coast are home to marine iguanas. They're the only lizards in the world that spend lots of time swimming in the salty ocean! They dive up to 33 feet (10 m) deep, scraping an underwater plant called *algae* (AL-jee) off of rocks. To warm up between dives in the cold ocean, the iguanas sun themselves on rocks.

To move fast, spiny-tailed and desert iguanas sometimes run on their two back legs.

Marine iguanas' bodies get rid of extra salt from the ocean by "sneezing" it out.

This marine iguana is searching for underwater algae to eat near the Galápagos Islands. Marine iguanas usually dive for only a few minutes. But if they need to, they can stay underwater a half-hour or longer.

11

This blue iguana is searching for food.

Caribbean islands are home to iguanas of all sizes, coloring, and ways of life. Some species live only on a single island. At over 5 feet (a meter and a half) long, blue iguanas are the biggest land animals on Grand Cayman. They are tan or grey with a bluish color—sometimes very blue! Odd-looking rhinoceros iguanas live in rocky coastal forests on Hispaniola. They get their name from the "horns" on their heads, which are actually turned-up scales. Fat pads on top of their heads and saggy muscles around their jaws add to their odd look. Jamaican iguanas live only on Jamaica. These iguanas have been nearly wiped out by hunters and by mongooses people brought to the island.

Jamaica's slow-moving, ground-living blue iguanas had no enemies until people brought cats and dogs to the island. Pet green iguanas that got loose now live on Jamaica, too. They can move more quickly, swim, and climb trees.

This rhinoceros iguana lives in the Dominican Republic. You can see the "horns" on its snout.

How Do Iguanas Live?

Iguanas that live in zoos or as pets gets lots of fresh fruits and greens. Some kinds also get a few crickets or mealworms as snacks.

Spiny-tailed iguanas have been known to eat bats, frogs, and birds—and even the eggs of their own kind. Local people like to eat these iguanas.

Iguanas eat mostly plant foods such as fruits and berries, tender young leaves, seeds, and flower buds. But some kinds also eat small amounts of animal foods such as bugs and grubs, dead birds or fish, land crabs, or eggs.

Like other cold-blooded reptiles, iguanas depend on outside warmth to warm their bodies. They spend a lot of time basking in the sun. If the sun is too hot, they need a shady place to cool down. Most iguanas live alone in a **territory** that has food, nice basking places, and a safe place to rest at night. Some males defend their territories so strongly that zoos cannot keep them with another male.

14

This iguana is munching on leaves in Costa Rica.

What Are Baby Iguanas Like?

Some kinds of iguanas grow up more quickly than others. It takes five to nine years for a rhinoceros iguana to become an adult.

A green iguana might lay 50 eggs—but only 3 to 10 of the babies will live to become adults.

Iguanas hatch from soft-shelled eggs. The mother finds a sunny spot and digs a burrow, then lays her eggs inside it. Depending on what kind of iguana she is, she might lay a few eggs, or dozens. She covers the burrow carefully and leaves. The sun helps keep the eggs warm. How soon the eggs hatch depends on the kind of iguana. After the new hatchlings break out of their shells, they dig their way out of the burrow. They are only a few inches long and are completely on their own! The babies face many dangers— including animals that want to eat them.

Here you can see two rhinoceros iguanas as they hatch in Puerto Rico.

16

Are Iguanas Dangerous?

Iguanas communicate by bobbing their heads, moving their bodies, sticking out their dewlaps, leaving smells, and hissing. These things often help iguanas avoid fighting.

Iguana teeth are triangular, with jagged edges. Whenever a tooth falls out, a new one takes its place.

Iguanas might look scary, but they're usually quite peaceful. Sometimes they fight with other iguanas. That's usually to protect their territories. Often they get their message across without actually fighting.

Iguanas also sometimes bite people who handle them or try to feed them. That's most likely when the iguanas aren't used to being around people, or when it's time for them to mate. Iguana bites are painful and can bleed heavily. The animals' small, sharp teeth are made for ripping plants. When people get bitten, they usually try to pull away. Then the teeth rip their flesh!

Here you can see two male marine iguanas fighting.

18

Like many other animals, iguanas can also carry disease-causing germs such as *Salmonella*. People who keep iguanas need to make sure the animals' living spaces stay clean. They need to wash up after handling the animals, too.

Iguanas can also be dangerous in another way. Sometimes people let them loose in places where they don't belong, turning them into **invasive** animals. Even if these newcomers don't hunt animals that belong there, they compete with them for food and living space and often harm plant life.

These invasive spiny-tailed iguanas are sunning themselves on Florida's Gasparilla Island.

Spiny-tailed iguanas from Mexico have gotten loose in Florida. Gasparilla Island has 12,000 of them! They eat people's gardens, nest in their attics, and weaken sand dunes with their burrows. They also carry diseases and eat eggs of tortoises and shorebirds.

21

Do Iguanas Make Good Pets?

People often put baby iguanas in a 10- or 20-gallon (38- to 76-liter) tank. But that's already too small, and the iguana will grow quickly. As a 6-foot (nearly 2-m) adult, it will need a large cage—or even an entire room.

A pet iguana might be free, but taking good care of it can cost a lot of money!

Iguanas—especially green iguanas—have become popular as pets. Some stores sell them for very little money. Fairs and carnivals sometimes give them away as prizes. But iguanas are not easy pets to care for!

A 6-inch (15-cm) green-iguana hatchling might look like a cute little pet. But in three years it will be 10 times that size! And it can easily live 15 or 20 years—longer than a dog. Iguanas need just the right lighting, temperature, food, living space, medical care, and attention. People often lose interest or do a poor job of taking care of these long-lived animals. If the iguanas are not kept clean and cared for properly, they get sick or die.

This boy is carefully holding a young green iguana.

There are other things to think about, too. Some iguanas are hand-raised to be pets. But others are caught in the wild, putting wild populations at risk. It's also hard to find homes for iguanas people no longer want. Zoos usually have all they need. Rescue groups try to help, but they can't find homes for all the extras. Some people turn pet iguanas loose outdoors. But releasing them where they don't belong is bad for the iguanas and also turns them into invasive species. Anyone who wants an iguana should learn a lot about these animals first, to make sure it's the right choice. It's also important to make sure the iguana was raised by people, not caught in the wild. And there are plenty of rescued iguanas still waiting for good homes.

This pet green iguana is keeping a close eye on the photographer.

People now bring about a million iguanas into the U.S. each year to sell as pets. Only a small number survive.

Wild-caught iguanas are more likely to carry diseases than ones people hatch and raise.

In most places it's illegal to turn animals loose—especially animals from other lands.

Are Iguanas in Danger?

In some places, endangered iguanas now get a head start. People raise them until they're old enough to stay safe from cats. Then they're released into the wild.

There are still lots of wild green iguanas. But some local populations are in danger from hunting, the pet trade, or habitat loss.

Many species of iguanas are **endangered**, or in danger of dying out. Other species are in trouble. One of the biggest reasons is loss of habitat. More people have moved into areas where iguanas live. Farming, logging, building, and other changes can destroy the iguanas' habitats. Some species are hunted heavily—sometimes illegally, by **poachers**. Some populations are harmed by people catching too many of the animals to sell as pets.

Many iguana species are harmed by invasive animals. That's especially true on many Caribbean islands. There, iguana eggs and young are eaten by people's cats, dogs, and other animals that now run loose. People's cattle also step on nests and eat plants the iguanas need for food. Invasive animals are a big reason why some Caribbean species are nearly **extinct**.

This wild green iguana lives near a harbor in Aruba. It must share its home with visitors, boats, and other machines.

Many people and governments are now working to save wild iguanas. They are trying to protect land areas where iguanas live and nest. They are getting local people interested in saving wild iguanas. They are teaching people to raise iguanas for food or pets instead of hunting wild ones. More programs now raise iguanas and add them to the wild population. And many places now have laws that limit killing iguanas or catching them to sell as pets.

We still have lots to learn about these interesting animals! No one knows whether some species of iguanas can still be saved. But careful planning and hard work might save many species that would otherwise die out. It would be nice to see iguanas munching on leaves, basking on rocks, climbing trees, or swimming in the ocean for many years to come!

This curious green iguana is peeking out of a plant in Honduras.

West Indian rock iguanas are some of the most endangered lizards in the world. Several of the species are nearly extinct.

Jamaican iguanas were thought to be extinct until a hunter's dog found one in 1990.

Keeping iguanas safe from invasive animals is a big part of helping

29

Glossary

endangered (in-DAYN-jurd) An endangered animal is one that is close to dying out completely. Many iguana species are endangered.

extinct (ek-STINKT) An extinct animal or plant is one that has completely died out. Some iguana species are nearly extinct.

habitats (HA-bit-tat) Animals' habitats are the types of surroundings in which the animals live. Iguanas live in a wide range of habitats.

invasive (in-VAY-siv) Invasive species are plants or animals that people bring to other lands, where they spread and harm other species. Many iguanas are killed by invasive animals.

lizard (LIH-zurd) A lizard is a reptile that has a long body, legs, and a long, pointed tail. Iguanas are lizards.

poachers (POH-churz) Poachers are people who kill wild animals illegally. Poachers kill many kinds of iguanas.

reptiles (REP-tylz) Reptiles are animals that have backbones, lungs, and tough skin covered with scales, and that need outside heat to warm their bodies. Iguanas are reptiles.

scales (SKAYLZ) Scales are small, hard plates that cover some animals' skin. Iguanas have scales.

species (SPEE-sheez) An animal species is a group of animals that share the same features and can have babies only with animals in the same group. There are many species of iguanas.

territory (TEHR-uh-tor-ee) An animal's territory is the area that the animal claims as its own and defends against outsiders. Most iguanas have territories.

To Find Out More

Read It!

Lockwood, Sophie. *Iguanas* (The World of Reptiles). The Child's World, 2006.

Miller, Jake. *The Green Iguana*. (The Lizard Library). New York: PowerKids Press, 2003.

Williams, Sarah. *101 Facts about Iguanas*. Milwaukee, WI: Gareth Stevens, 2001.

On the Web

Visit our Web page for lots of links about iguanas: *http://www.childsworld.com/links*

Note to Parents, Teachers, and Librarians: We routinely check our Web links to make sure they're safe, active sites—so encourage your readers to check them out!

31

Index

About the Author

Kathryn Stevens is an archaeologist as well as an editor and author of numerous children's books on nature and science, geography, and other topics. She lives in western Wisconsin, where she spends her spare time enjoying the outdoors, restoring a Victorian house, and making pet-therapy visits with her dog.